D1740143

# Myracle's Journey

## Woven with Ribbons and Pearls

## A Mother's Perspective

Regina Woodard Cannon

Outskirts Press, Inc.
http://www.outskirtspress.com

ISBN: 978-1-4787-6229-4

Outskirts Press and the "OP" logo are trademarks belonging to Outskirts Press, Inc.

PRINTED IN THE UNITED STATES OF AMERICA

# Dedications

Dr. Juel Pate Borders (who cared for me during a very difficult pregnancy)Myracle's middle name is Juel after Dr. Borders.

Dr. Runette Flowers (who cared for Myracle from the first breath to the last)

Mr. Leophas Aubrey Woodard, my daddy, who was the "captain" of our ship. He made sure we were "always" there for each other.

Ms. Joycelyn Woodard Hunt (my darling sister#2) who was Myracle's first Mom for seven days and also her God-Mother). Thanks for giving her your love and spoiling her rotten.

Ms. Toni Woodard Thomas (my loving sister #5) who listened and used her creativity to design the cover.

Ms. Myra Woodard Jenkins, (my caring sister #6) who was Myracle's live in baby sitter and who often told her to behave.


Thanks to all of you for all of your love and support!

# Table of Contents

# *Author's Note*

This is a work of non-fiction displayed by the mother, Regina Woodard Cannon. It is my recollection, reconstructed from my experience during Myracle's lifespan April 30 1984 – February 7, 1986.

For many years, I struggled with how to tell her story. It was always my intention to write 21 threads to reflect her life span .

Today, I can truthfully say, it has been a long and arduous process. I clearly see the ribbons and pearls of Myracle's Journey and I am encouraged.

*"I believe the nicest and sweetest days are not shoes on which anything very splendid or wonderful or exciting happens, but just those that bring simple little pleasures, following one another softly, like pearls off a string."*

*Unknown*

# *Myracle's Journey*

On August 10, 1983, love entered into my heart and it was a miracle. I had never felt like this. It was magical and the entire world was aglow. I walked, talked, shouted with this gift of life and love that transcended my body. Of course, the agony of a four day rest in bed found no splendor. Tests were being run to determine the accuracy of the feeling within my heart for this special love. Was I really going to have a baby?

I remembered to rely on GOD for assurance. He gives and takes and in the back of my mind, I knew that he could only create "miracles". As time passed by, the evolution of his wonders to perform lingered and encapsulated me. Early one morning about a week later the telephone rang, and the person asked if this was Ms. Cannon? Without a doubt, I responded, yes! The caller was Mrs. Wynn (the nurse) from Dr. Juel Borders' office. She said, the results were "positive". This was great news to my tender ears. I sat up with a big heroic smile on my face and asked, are you sure? Well, yes said the caller in a soft spoken voice, there's no doubt. There is a fetus. My reply, "Oh Lord", it's a miracle and I'll name her MYRACLE.

Throughout the trials and heartaches of the pregnancy due to my age, I knew that Myracle would make it to term and be here soon. I could feel that she was feisty and very much alive during the nine months. I always had a sense of so much joy and love. Without a doubt we were making plans for her future. (Not uncommon for parents) and everybody else in my family.

Of course, I had many battles with the pregnancy and I felt Myracle's determination with every kick. Many, many tests and precautionary measures were always in abundance. Do this and don't do that! With all of this fuss I never broke one commandment of the pregnancy. I had previously been told that I would NEVER be able to conceive. This was disheartening especially since I strived so hard in my personal, professional and educational pursuits. Surely this was indeed my time for motherhood. This child was to be a real blessing. Somehow, I never really imagined being complete without motherhood even with 6 siblings (all girls). It is not the same.

Truly, God answers prayers and provides needs. The months and days passed and they were becoming more and more exciting as I carried Myracle. What a happy time. When I told anyone what her name would be, oddly enough there were all kinds of responses.

My brother-in-law, Marshall said, "They will call her miracle whip". And when she goes to school she will be teased. Other people said I was crazy to give her that name. So be it...

In the seventh (7) month my contractions were so severe I had to be hospitalized.

I also developed influenza. It was a very delicate and catastrophic period for me. Myracle was just holding on. Sometimes I meditated and counted my blessings. Two more months and it will be over. Surprisingly I did not know she would be a girl. What an assumption? I just believed. After all, my daddy "Leo" had seven girls. I am the first born daughter so it was fitting for me. I enjoyed the "frills" of girly things like my mama Catherine. The practice of always babysitting was going to be natural.

> *"Each day comes bearing its own gifts, Untie the ribbons."*
>
> *Ruth Ann Schabacker*

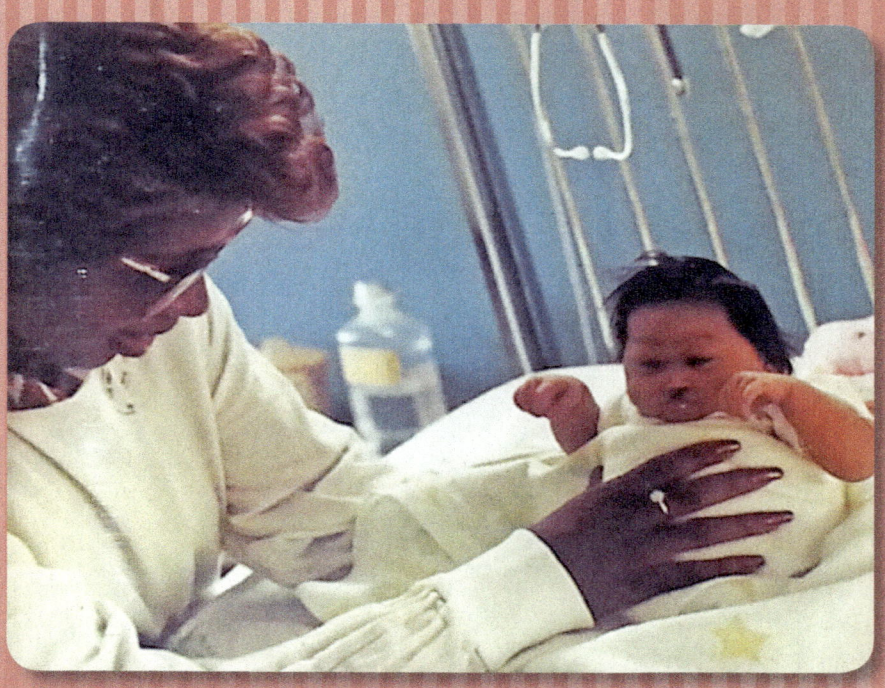

**Myracle being held by Nanny Joyce at 2 days old**

# 1 THREAD

## *She's Coming*

The time drew closer and we waited for some sign to drive to the hospital. It was on April 30, 1984 at 7:00am and I had walked the long halls back and forth in our Victorian home several times with very excruciating pain. I knew it was time so I proceeded to shower and dress. We called Dr. Borders and met her at the hospital at 8:00am. My contractions were 1.5 centimeters apart and the pain was quite severe and I could not breathe.

After 15.5 hours, the doctors decided to perform a caesarian. Myracle was born at 11:50pm on April 30, 1984 weighing 7 lbs. and 19 inches long at Southwest Hospital, Atlanta, Georgia.

Soon after my recovery, I remembered talking to a lot of nurses and doctors and perhaps other hospital staff. It was late and I was groggy. I heard people talking and somebody was holding my hands for about 10 minutes. I heard noise but was clueless as to what it was. The room was bombarded with people. I heard them tell me there had been severe complications and Myracle was being transported by helicopter to Egleston Hospital. Someone said, let her see her because she may not make it.

I did not understand… several days later the story was told. Myracle may not survive! She has brain-damage, holoprosencephaly, cleft-lip, one nostril and underdeveloped ability in motor skills… she's extremely retarded. She is being monitored, etc.

My Lord, as a librarian, I began to pray, read and research the literature while confined to my hospital bed. I was in Southwest Atlanta and Myracle was 20 miles away fighting for her life. Of course, with these thoughts, everybody said she was beautiful. My sister, Chubby(Joycelyn) arrived immediately and stayed with Myracle at Egleston. I guess my daddy, Leo told her to get to Atlanta. When she arrived Myracle was extremely monitored. Every sigh, grin, smile, move, weight, etc. during the entire seven days we were apart. Myracle wore barrettes at 2 days old. The girly trend has started…match, match, match!

Well, I continued to pray and so did the doctors and nurses as well as my family that she would live long enough for me to really see and hold her for myself. Seven days later, on May 7, 1984, I left Southwest Hospital in a wheelchair to go and get my baby from Egleston. It was an ordeal waiting about 4 hours to check her out but we managed. She was lovely and with a full spirit. I cannot begin to explain how I felt, although I knew in my heart she was a fighter, just like her mom.

Myracle was assigned 24 hour nurses to go home with us to assist in relieving some of the pressures. During this process, I learned that holoprosencephaly; the true diagnosis was that these babies do not live beyond 8 months to a year. Statistically, none have survived any longer. They do not eat and the picture became more glim.

This is really hard to decipher. However, I could see Myracle was stubborn and had a mind of her own. She was a real challenge. So I went on a mission, to prove she would do the opposite of the medical predictions. After all, there were no real statistics. Let's call this a mother's intuition!

Because of her cleft-lip, she could only use a lamb's nipple and drink very slowly. Her bottle was a gold medicine bottle that looked like an old paregoric bottle.

I learned a few tricks by pinching large holes in it so that it would not take her 4 hours to suck an ounce of milk. I programmed myself to adjust. Thank God for rocking chairs and good lungs to sing. Of course, after a week of rocking and holding she became quite spoiled. Consequently, at home, she wanted the same rock me treatment. The nurses at Egleston thought she was a doll and she was constantly rocked. Yes, Myracle had special needs and everybody succumbed to all of her whims.

Even with her challenges, she was treated as if she was a bright and normal child. True, she showed some signs of normalcy. But, she was mentally and physically retarded. She had temperaments just like a normal child especially when it came to sleeping. She always wanted to stay awake all night.

During the transition, we took shifts while caring for her with the intent of breaking her little routine but it never worked. When most children were asleep, she was bright eyed and bushy tailed with loads of entertainment.

To break some of the routine, we literally pulled straws every night to see who would have the **night** shift because any way you look at it… there would be challenges. Somebody and or nobody would get any rest. Between the walking, humming and singing everything was for Myracle. Sometimes it was joyous and humorous at the same time. With Myracle, we took the bitter with the sweet. Seriously, I was always tired but it was a good tired.

The harder I worked, the more Myracle wanted to show out. She never showed signs of wanting anything. She was just needy! She had me wrapped around her finger. I could never get over her big wide smile.

> *"We cannot live only for ourselves. A thousand fibers connect us with our fellow men; and among those fibers, as sympathetic threads, our actions run as causes, and they come back to us as effects."*
>
> *Herman Melville*

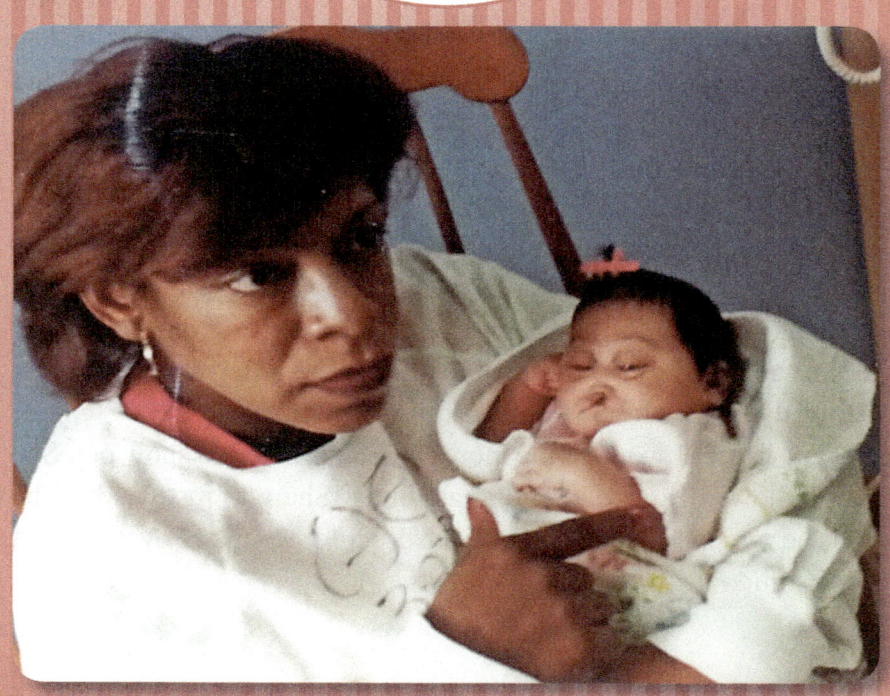

**Mommy holding Myracle for the first time**

# 2 THREADS

## *Personality Development*

Iremember telling myself not to trust her unless she was asleep. Her favorite activity was scooting and turning from side to side in the bed. Well, by the fifth day I had worn myself thin. When I held her she was somewhat listless, so I called the doctor. As you know, we were back in the hospital for observation. We stayed there for another week and came home on Mother's Day. Again, the agony of her life span was uttered coutless times. As a result, the Mobile, Alabama and Mississippi family members came for the reckoning of her fate. What an ordeal.

It was beginning to be a nightmare. I received so many opinions from the doctors because no one had any expertise. Yet, I maintained my own convictions. Finally, I had had enough and just wanted to let everybody know about Myracle, my daughter, the person. Unlike most diagnosis of HPE, each case is entirely different and there are no comparisons or statistics only speculations.

Knowing how difficult Myracle's care was, I began to chart her course. At some point it was down to a science. I recorded everything because it was always so much uncertainty with her demeanor. No one believed me if it was not recorded and I did not want to chance my memory.

If she gained weight, experienced signs of real hunger or was overly agitated it was always noted. As a matter of fact, one night, Myracle was only 1.5 months (I thought she was hungry) so, I mixed formula and rice cereal, grabbed a spoon and fed her. She ate all of it and afterwards went to sleep and had several burps. Amazing as it was, Myracle was not supposed to eat from a spoon. I informed the doctor about the feeding and she told me to proceed. Yeah, progress!!! She even opened her mouth for more. Only through his grace and his mercy! Many times I just tried different things because it was not textbook knowledge. It was always trial and error to make something happen for Myracle.

*Ask and it shall be given you.*

*Matthew 7:7*

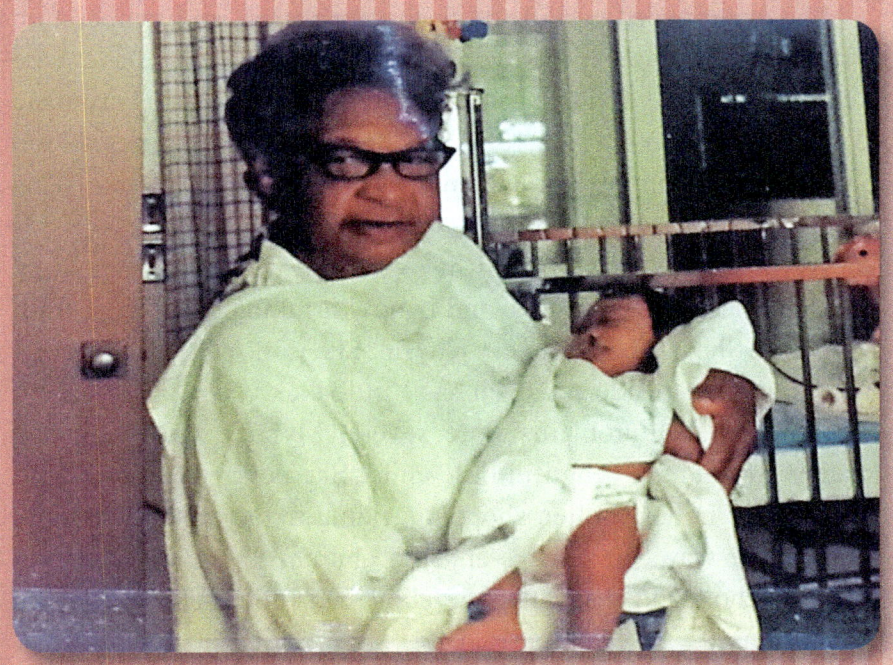

**Granny holding Myracle**

# 3 THREADS

*Searching for Normalcy*

Two months later, Myracle was christened with all of the festive trimmings at Shaw Temple A.M.E. Zion Church.

She experienced periods of sleep deprivation, and temperature fluctuations because of the hypothalamus irregularities. Days were a combination of good and bad for Myracle. Another trip was made to the hospital on July 23,1984, to check the irregularities, blood count and medicines . Yes, and another 6 day stay at Egleston. This is beginning to be our home.

At three months, Myracle was rotten and wanted to be held by anyone. She weighed 11 lbs. and is now drinking rice cereal from her bottle. She has become very playful. She is moving her arms and head from side to side and even has a little kick.

Although her problems were severe, Myracle was without a shadow of doubt, a beautiful little child. She never went unnoticed either while in her stroller, shopping, riding in the car or at church. And by the way, she always enjoyed church. She hummed along with the choir and long after the choir had finished singing. This was so funny!

At first, I would put my hand over her mouth because she was loud. The minister told me not to do it anymore, just let her be.

During the preaching, she would always be asleep, no amens from her because she usually missed the word. A good thing!!! Now, at the end of service, she was always awake because she knew everyone would be there to kiss and hold her. Yes, she was something else... quite amusing too.

There were many signs of "normalcy", as Myracle aged. But I knew signs of the retardation would become more obvious. This I could not understand, but I listened intently on the possibility of placing her in a rehabilitation facility. The search for a rehabilitation facility became a frightening monster. How could I do this? This is my child and this is not an easy task. True, her seizures were mild, never any grandmas . I learned over time that I could talk her out of any seizure with just a few loving words and by holding her hands. I just told her, NO Myracle...let's not do that! It was a calming process for me too and I guess I found the trigger points and words to use on her. It worked.

Most of the time Myracle was obedient, yet very strong willed to do what she wanted to do whether right or wrong. She managed to have her way. Somehow, she proved everybody wrong in diagnosing her case. As a part of the process, I researched and interviewed many agencies regarding her care.

I was determined not to send my baby away. This was a very difficult situation. To offset some of this, we just tried to be normal. We really practiced being normal.

For instance, Myracle and I often went to church, walked to the parks, grocery shopped, or just strolled around the neighborhood. She fussed because she did not like to be confined. As a matter of fact, she never wanted to sit in a shopping buggy or stroller. She wanted me to hold her as I walked around. How insane was that?

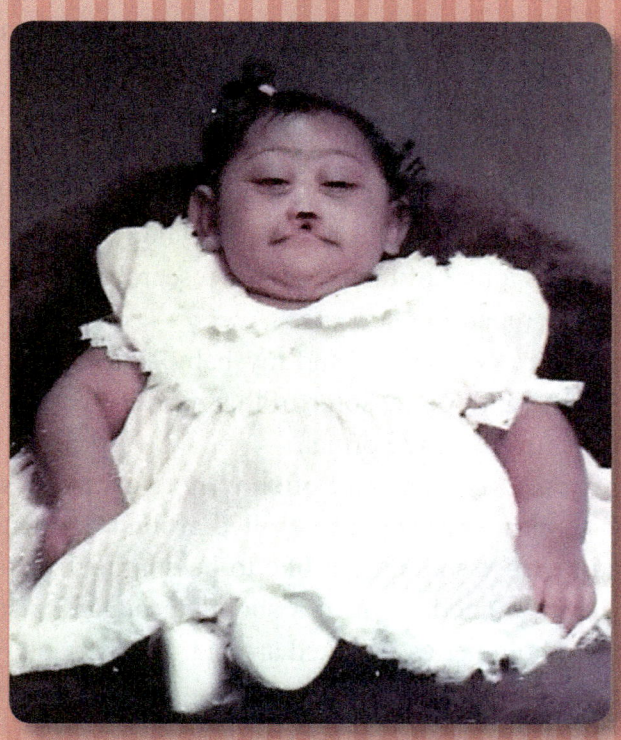

**Myracle posing at 3 months**

# 4 THREADS

## *Reunion Times*

In August, we are planning a trip out of town for a family reunion, by car. To our surprise she was wonderful. We attended a picnic and of course she slept. And she was awake all night. Not unusual for her. We enjoyed the festivities. During the trip, she got her ears pierced and did not cry and neither do I. However, Nanny Joyce cried.

Another milestone, Myracle began to eat vegetables and I believe she liked them. Overall, she is adjusting very well and the routine of pampering, diapering, rocking, temperature fluctuations is becoming a thing of the past.

At four and a half months, Myracle has a boyfriend and his name is Quentin. They are about six weeks apart in age. She takes pictures with Quentin and makes goo goo eyes at each other. He also pulls her hair.

I decided to go back to work after 5 months but with much hesitation about leaving Myracle. On the first day back, I went home at lunch to get a hug and a kiss and then I cried for leaving her. I tried something different and played her some music. I noticed whenever she heard music there is this calming about her. From that day forward I never turned off the radio.

Now it's time to take a family portrait. Off to Olan Mills and Myracle is a trip; not cooperating. As you would know, she's asleep and her hair needs to be brushed. We enter the room and place cold towels to her face in an effort to arouse her, but to no avail. We wait about 15 minutes and notice a stir. The cameraman is superb! He brings toys and yells and the child becomes bright-eyed for the pose. What excitement! She is having her way once again.

With Myracle, there is never a dull moment around the house. We visit friends, and Myracle sleeps. According to the doctors , all sleep activities must be monitored. When she sleeps that's it and always at the wrong time, especially during the day.

At night her entertainment was always original…whatever, just go for it!

*"In knowing how to overcome little things, a centimeter at a time, gradually when big things come, you are prepared."*

*Katherine Dunham*

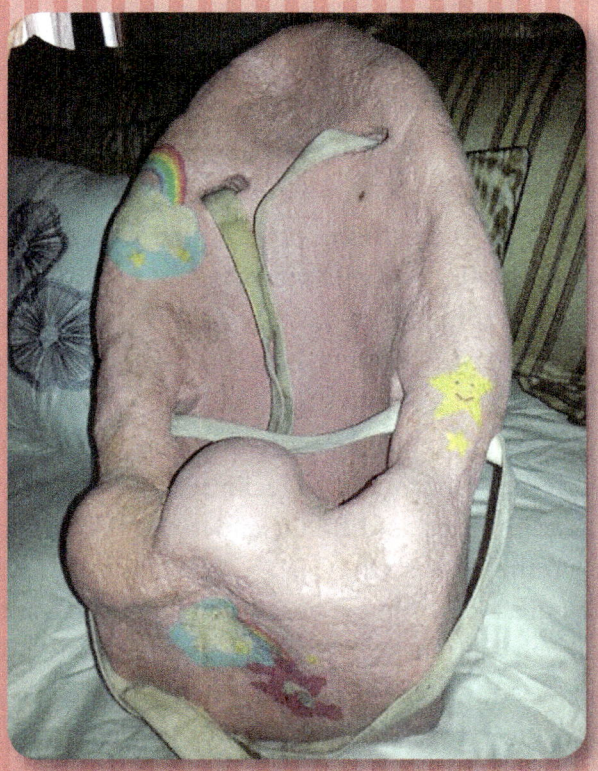

**Myracle's special designed seat**

# 5 THREADS

## *Trial and Error*

Six months later, I am on the blink from being tired but I can't give up. I must go on because Myracle is such a joy and definitely "special". We decided to place her at Georgia Retardation Center in October but with much hesitancy. It is twenty-two miles, one-way from our home. We visit every day and Myracle comes home every Friday. It's a timing process, but no one can care or attempt to care for your child like you can.

GRC is a gruesome place and Myracle is the youngest child at the center of about 360 patients. She is in the hospital unit for special care. I hate the idea and all of those in authority. I don't feel there is any love or commitment offered in the center from the doctors and the degree of trust is also lacking.

Yes, the adjustment is difficult and I can't forgive myself for sending her to that place. Oh, GOD… Unhappy with the situation, we try to obtain a service to get her placed back into our home. Gee, there is so much red tape and red flags and the State always WIN. Case after case ,and letter after letter, we could not get a precedence from a prior Katie-Becket decision but we continued to fight! Appeal after appeal, we came out the losers every time.

*"Life is to be lived, not controlled, and humanity is won by continuing to play in face of certain defeat."*

*Ralph Ellison*

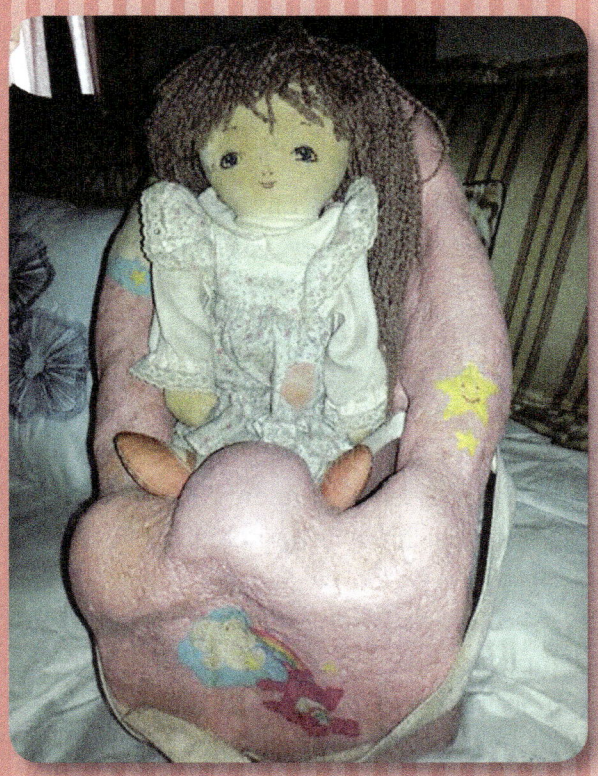

**Myracle's Raggedy Ann doll in her seat**

# 6 THREADS

## The Holidays

The holiday season is approaching. We decided to go and take pictures with Santa. There again, Myracle gets her normal stress, can't be still in Santa's lap but we manage to get her adjusted and that wholesome smile appears. People applaud and tell her how pretty she is. So goes the story… on the way home she falls asleep.

A few days later, we journey with high hopes to Mobile for Christmas. Myracle Juel slept all the way, a 5 hour drive from Atlanta. The weather was absolutely perfect at 72 degrees and Myracle could not stand the heat. That part of her brain definitely does not regulate. Therefore she had to change clothes twice before reaching a comfort level. Unlike the other family members who were dressed, decked out for the holidays, Myracle wore only her diaper and t-shirt. The beautiful red dress just hung in the closet. Oh well, so much for fashion.

Of course, she adjusted pretty well for a 7 month old and was really quite bright eyed. She received lots of toys and clothes and was very happy going from arm to arm; her usual.

We brought in the New Year at church with Myracle. We saw many relatives and friends. On the way home, Myracle did not want to sit in her car seat and I had to pull off the road for some arm holding. She gets to have her way!

There were loads of challenges; and I realized she was very curious and I started to read to her and show her books and pictures. This was a calming sigh for an 8 month old, supposedly severely handicapped and undeveloped brain child. But her motor skills were not as prevalent. Myracle constantly tried and usually managed in her own way. She was stubborn and would always do what she wanted to do. Just a real piece of work and my pride and joy! With her frailty, I did not trust her enough to ignore her whims but I was sometimes firm. Not that it really mattered, she would "smile" after I told her what to do. Imagine? Many times I would just laugh because she never made me angry. Her strength was most encouraging because I would always be there for her.

Mentally I was programmed to believe "Myracle" had severe problems and there was no hope! Somehow those thoughts did not resonate and we knew that my faith and love we for her never stigmatized my belief in her ability. At this age and stage in her life, there were supposed to be a tremendous deterioration and ultimate death by now… but Myracle was a living testimony that life must go on. With this knowledge and so called facts, her doctors were shocked that she was still here; alive and making unbelievable progress.

*"Our lives begin to end the day we become silent about things that matter."*

*Martin Luther King Jr.*

**Myracle's Nipple**

# 7 THREADS

## *Hoping for Tomorrow*

Making plans for Myracle was as if there would always be a "tomorrow" because she was strong and quite vivacious. She had her first tooth at 8.34 months old and she looked like a little doll. Her tomorrows were always precious moments. We went to church almost every Sunday and of course, Myracle always had a ball singing, sleeping during the sermon, going from person to person and always waking up before church was over. In this way, she would be available for her many hugs and kisses. She was called "Miss America" because she was always dressed so cute. Just because she was handicapped did not make her any less beautiful because she always smiled, jumped and looked around to see everything. My girl....

Whether she actually could see was never determined; however it was evident some sight was present. Her sense of touch, smell and sound was definitely not impaired. She would jolt, just like a normal child if there was loud noise. She really enjoyed music. I would let her stand and sometimes there was a twist but not like "Chubby Checker".

> *"Humankind has not woven the web of life. We are but one thread within it. Whatever we do to the web, we do to ourselves. All things are bound together. All things connect."*
>
> *Unknown*

**Myracle and Santa**

# 8 THREADS

## *Perfect Easter*

Easter is fast approaching and more plans are being made for Myracle.

For so long, Egleston Hospital was a big part of our life. As a matter of fact, we entered the hospital two weeks before Easter. We came home the Saturday before Easter but not without getting Myracle an Easter basket from the hospital. I picked up her designed peach dress, adorned with lace and ribbons.

The dress was designed by Joan's House of Couture. As a part of the design process, Myracle went for two fittings. She acted just like a big girl while her measurements were being taken. It was so much fun. The design of her dress contained 6 yards of fabric, 5 yards of lining, 25 yards of lace and 15 yards of bows and it was only 13 inches long. A hunk of a dress. It was truly amazing! She was a perfect peach doll.!!

On Easter Sunday morning, I wanted everything to be PERFECT because it was a real chore to get Myracle prepared with all of the frill. The hair was unruly and nothing would hold the pony tails, barrettes, ribbons or rubber bands. The perfect style never came so I gave up and went on to something else.

It took about 15 minutes to put on the dress and tie all the ribbons at the sleeves, around the neck line and at the waist. I called on JESUS! I went back and forth with her hair again but that proved to be unruly. I was really tired.

Finally, Myracle was also tired and on the way to church she acted gracious. While sitting there, within 30 minutes, her eyes became very heavy and the little one slept throughout the Easter service. When she sat in my lap, her dress was all over the place. Afterwards, we posed for pictures and her eyes were without a doubt closed. I just held her in my arms and the cameras snapped. Poor baby never heard any of the glorious comments about how she looked in that beautiful designed dress. She may not have even cared.

The designer Joan said, she had never constructed or fitted anyone so small. We felt fortunate!! Furthermore, she said, never again! It was like making something for a baby doll and she weighed only 14 pounds. Truly Amazing!!!

I could not ask for more. My precious baby is a real "jewel".

*"At the core of life is a hard purposefulness, a determination to live."*
*Howard Thurman*
American theologian, clergyman and activist.
1900-1981

**Just being good**

# 9 THREADS

## *Admiration*

Yes, Myracle was an unusual child. She attended birthday parties and even had her first trip on a sliding board and was not afraid. She enjoyed the outdoors but not like being in her stroller. Usually, I ended up carrying her and pushing the stroller, especially when going shopping or walking in the park. Most people just stared, stopped and talked. Sometimes I could tell there were questions just from the look on their faces. Why was I out in public with her; this funny looking child?

Little children especially, just wanted to know why she looked so strange. They asked, can she be fixed? My reply, God made her this way and they were satisfied Sometimes I said, once she gets older she may look different. Other times, folk just said, I admire you. Usually, if *the person had previously seen us together,* their remarks were minimal. And the second and or third chance meeting it was, oh, hi Myracle. She would give that infectious smile with the little pegs between the cleft lips. She was as cute as pie. I cannot begin to tell you about her innocence. She relished attention.

Because she was "special", different, most people were just in awe. It took the courage of a little girl in church to make a difference. She presented a paper to her class about Myracle.

In the presentation, she described how Myracle looked, her uniqueness in sucking a lamb's nipple and her response to situations. She adored Myracle and told everyone she was her little sister, often showing her pictures to everyone. What admiration and honesty. Truths are always told from a child's heart.

Many of her pictures were displayed in children's specialty shops and usually little kids would say, "There's Myracle" .And it was joyous to hear. With her looks, there was never mockery. Apparently people just looked with an inquiring mind .I guess they were just thinking. Some folk actually said, I want to be a miracle when I told them her name. What admiration? Priceless!

Sometimes she would have seizures and I just gently talked to her. I called her name, Myracle, let's not do that. Other times, I would squeeze her hands and the seizure would magically disappear. A part of the reality check was to prove this was possible. So, from time to time, I had to actually perform the special technique for her doctors' .They were amazed and so was I.

It is hard to phantom. She came into the world with doubts and now she has personality. Myracle is a true blessing. She is a gifted child who is surrounded by the love of family. She senses that love and she is not the exception. I admire her strives and character because she exemplifies hope.

Yes, she was always surrounded by people who cared. I worked in a college as a Librarian at the time and it was nothing strange for Myracle to come to school, visit and disturb the classes. My students adored her. She always came "first" in my life. Her purpose was my purpose…to be still and know. There were always bitter and sweet days. I vowed to move on because I knew miracles would be coming. She was a true testament to life.

*"Commit to the Lord
whatever you do,
and your plans will succeed."*

*Proverbs 16:3*

**Designer dress by Joan Robinson**

# 10 THREADS

## *Beating the Odds*

After many months of research, it seemed evident Myracle would live beyond expectations. She had her first birthday party and it was a big affair. There were 17 kids and 24 adults present, as well as a professional photographer. The entire house was decorated with hundreds of balloons and streamers , all for the birthday girl.

There was plenty of food and Myracle had a beautiful strawberry short cake. The "honoree" wore pink, smiled and sat in her strapped car seat and surprisingly stayed awake for the entire party. She was absolutely wonderful and even attempted to blow out her 1 candle, of course, with my assistance.

It was a happy day for all of us especially since Myracle has made the one (1) year mark of her life. Somehow that dark cloud faded and the real gist of her being was becoming a reality! There was a big sigh. I no longer had this fear about losing her because she made it perfectly clear she would be able to manage the obstacles ahead. She was beating the odds.

There was no longer the nervous tension she would soon die. It was time to just live and fight. I took some deep breaths and learned to make more adjustments because she wanted to live and learn and so did I.

She has beaten the odds. She has started to grow more and get teeth. Instead of becoming fragile, she blossomed. A few colds, lowering of levels and even pneumonia did not seem to have a profound effect upon her desire to thrive, to live and be that shining star.

In many cases, the fact of her longevity became less important because I was determined to make everyday a blessing. I just wanted to have fun. I became more protective and sometimes it was sickening. I just wanted the best for Myracle.

I even fired two nurses because they (1) ignored her and the other one did not keep her nose cleaned; an important factor necessary for her breathing. With one nostril, how could one be so careless?

I became so fanatical , sometimes I pretended to be the doctor. Well, I am not stupid and the fact that I am a Librarian by profession has certainly been an asset. When it comes to Myracle, and HPE problems, you can best believe if it was to be found, I researched and read it. After all , what is a challenge? I had no fear of loss or uncertainty because my focus was always Myracle.

My friends were at CDC, NIH and Research Triangle Park in North Carolina. I am about a mission of discovery. There must be some rhyme and reason behind her multiplicities of disabilities.

> *"Do everything in love."*
>
> *1 Corinthians 16:14*

**Me, Granddaddy Leo and Myracle**

# 11 THREADS

## *Blessed with a Purpose*

Iknow from experience and research that Myracle came into this world blessed and with a purpose to fulfill. Often times, we sit and judge a person by the amount of time they spend on earth, instead of looking at their good deeds.

I am a very demanding mom and would usually receive much static when it came to preferential treatment for her. A day never passed that I did not drive the 22 miles one way to see her. Having worked an 8 hour day did not preclude me from seeing my child. That rarely happened.

Many times I would stay until 10, 11 or 12pm at night, then travel home. I never left unless she was asleep. If I tried, the world would be turned upside down for her. Myracle's agitation was like nothing anyone could imagine .All of the good girl nicety vanished. For me there was no turning back! I had to be in for the long haul and deal with the upheavals.

Every night I called back to the center before going to bed. It was so crazy. I would set the clock for 2am or 3am to check on her and call again immediately upon rising in the morning. I never trusted those who cared for her, especially the 11pm-7am shift. I had to monitor them and literally worry about Myracle.

It was a constant thing. Sometimes her seizures would become so bad; she would receive phenobarbital dose injections. However, if my instructions were followed many of her problems would be lessened. I kept a log of her activities. There was a known strategy to dose her up and she would become as limp as a dish rag. When she was in this state it was no fun for me or for her. We usually had to play the wait and see game; never knowing the impact of her meds. Sometimes she was okay and other times it could prove not so good.

I constantly stressed that I was her mother and not a medical expert. On the other hand, I knew her better than any doctor or nurse. She did not receive any medications during her weekend stays at home, Friday- Sunday.

At times when I felt like it, Myracle would come home any day of the week. Sometimes she would not go back to that dreadful place until Monday or Tuesday of the following week... After all, she was my child. I just signed her out and went home. This was really a difficult position. There was this constant stance to always prove what was in her best interest. There was no question, "I knew how to care for her" and she was never without arms to hold her. I could always call in the village for support.

Unlike most of the other patients in the skill-1 unit, Myracle was the only child who came home every week-end, and of course, all holidays.

There was no question, she was coming home. Aside from being spoiled, she was the youngest child at the center.

Everybody knew Myracle, the security guards, people from the kitchen, the cleaning crew, everybody came to see her. When I arrived, often times I was teased about my next reaction. I wanted all of her reports for the day. What was her demeanor? Did she eat? How much did she sleep? What were her medical dosages? Etc... Had she been a good or naughty girl? Just the normal schedule... with all of the T's, dots, and I's. It was a mother's prerogative.

Myracle was always showing out. The staff had asked me to allow her to participate in the fashion show. Not really sure how blessed she was at this point but I agreed. I took off from work and told everybody about the event. She was dressed in a beautiful powder blue pant suit with matching ribbons and bows. What was her talent? I guess it was my carrying her across the stage to model her outfit. She smiled without hesitation.

Poor baby, I did not want her to become agitated and so she slept in her chair until it was time to actually perform. What a cutie!

The truth of the matter, she was in my arms and we walked the so called runway. She was bright eyed and bushy tailed for the event. I was amazed! She won 3$^{rd}$ place in the Special Olympics. Myracle had become a star!

I always knew she was a handful and she could become quite manipulative. Sometimes Myracle would seek attention while at the center. The aides, and nurses would have to take her to lunch with them because she did not want to stay in her bed. A spoiled little brat. Brenda , another aide could not leave her because everywhere she went Myracle thought she should be with her. Just having her way…

It became so difficult at times that she would not allow anyone to feed her except Brenda. Then, there was another nurse from whom she would not even take her bottle. As a result, she was permanently assigned to Brenda. This child developed a sense of confidence and would even permit Brenda to tell her to "shut" up and "go to sleep".

Yes, she responded. By the way, aside from me and my sister, Myra who lived with me, Brenda was the only person who had ever baby sat Myracle. Sometimes I needed to run an uninterrupted errand and I would drop her off at Brenda's house and not even worry. After all, Myracle knew she was in good hands. Brenda named her daughter Myracle.

> *"Don't ask what the world needs. Ask what makes you come alive, and go do it. Because what the world needs are people who have come alive."*

*Howard Thurman*
American theologian,
clergyman and activist.
1900-1981

**Myracle on Easter Sunday**

# 12 THREADS

## *Making Laughs*

Now, under normal standards Myracle was not capable of interactions. She was never to do anything **normal** because she was handicapped and "quite retarded". Well, she had limits and extremes just like you and I. She was able to be controlled and manipulated like any normal human being.

Remember, she is a baby, not a monster. Had I been any other kind of parent I would have been afraid of my own child, but I was not. Aside from the challenges, my job was to make her comfortable and feel loved. I had no problem with her mental or physical appearance because she was **my** "special "child. Everybody's born with something and some things are seen and others are unseen.

Myracle made me laugh when I thought that she was getting away with murder. I remember distinctly leaving her in the crib and walking away for about 10 minutes to give her time to fuss. I really felt bad and so did Myracle at the time; however, when I went to peep, she hushed. I smiled and picked her up. Hey that's what she wanted and that's what I did. I gave in…

On another occasion, I had to prepare dinner and she did not want to sit in her walker, so we negotiated. Can you imagine?

I peeled carrots and cooked with her on my hips. I had no choice.

Another day, she would not go to sleep so we played, read and sang until 4:30pm. The child was unreal. She did not want me out of her sight. Naughty, Naughty…She generated more laughs…what else could I do? There is no harm in having your way or having your say.

*"Change will not come if we wait for some other person or some other time. We are the ones we've been waiting for. We are the change that we seek."*

*Barack Obama –*
44th President of the United States

**Baptismal Sunday**

# 13 THREADS

## *One Day at a Time*

Myracle's journey felt just like make believe. Many times she wanted to play and not sleep. She would go to bed and sleep until 9:00 am. The first time it happened, I jumped up at 7:00 am, ran to her room, peeped and jumped back into bed. Then I remembered, I did not check to see if she was still breathing. The excitement was uncontrollable; so I jumped up very quickly, ran back and yes, she was alright.

I got a big laugh out of that and I was in shock. Gee, I said, thank God!

I remembered to take one day at a time and when she's awake there is always a new beginning. I am quietly listening. There are little sounds surrounding the room and Myracle is noisy. It's time to move. No rest for the weary!

The daily chores are about to begin: soak, mash, chop medicines, measure, get thermometer, prepare bottle, food, bath, clothes… and on and on… It's a mad house! Why? When Myracle wakes up the world turns and she wants to be held.

Never mind about the preparations because it is so hard to stay ahead of her whims.

It's what you call constant. To take a breath is a delight and

Myracle wants to play and turn into a raisin while in the bathtub. Man oh man! She loves to get her hair washed. The water flowing makes her silly. She loves it.

But to get dressed, is an ordeal. I lay out her garments. Everything has to match from head to toe and there must be ribbons in the hair at all times. She must have matching socks even at bed time to match her pajamas and no exception. Crazy and simple. People thought I was crazy.

Admittedly, I was a fanatic and Myracle enjoyed being pampered. She always lost a ribbon or barrette. Sometimes she was a real mess and all the pampering in the world had been a waste of time. I would just chuckle and ask Myracle if she cared? She just smiled. It was just another day. So much for being prissy…

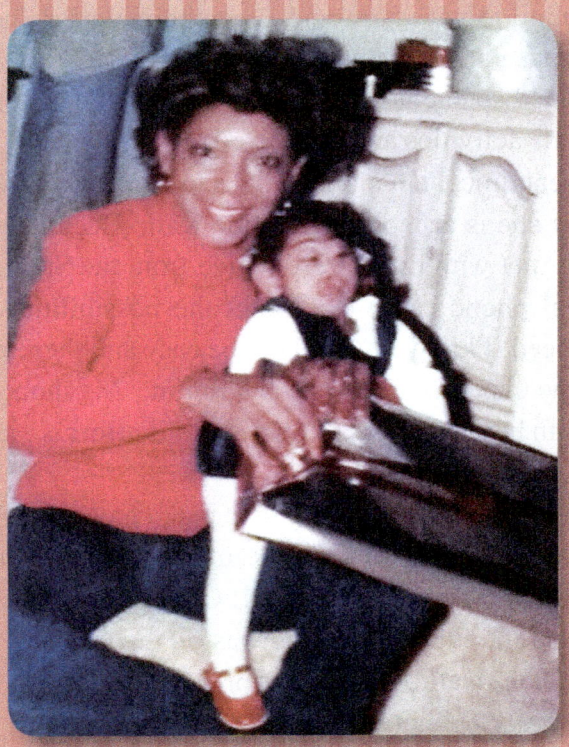

**Christmas Excitement**

# 14 THREADS

## *Throwing Away the Nipple*

It's beginning to get warm and I am shopping for shorts and culottes because she can't stand the heat. Myracle's hypothalamus is not regulated so she is always a bit warm. Whenever we go out, sometimes the activities are short lived.

In the meantime, I am making plans to have her taken away from the center. If she is accepted under the Katie-Beckett waiver I will be thrilled. I met with the representative from the State Department (after several phone calls) to discuss the possibilities. A red tape situation indeed! I knew it would not be easy and therefore prepared myself for the unnecessary hassle and routine. My thoughts, nothing is really worth having unless a conscientious effort is made. I played the waiting game with the State.

In the meantime, Myracle began to make progress in other areas. It was taking a long time to get milk into her so I tried using a regular nipple with her bottle. Hallelujah!! Of course, there were about 4 holes punched into the nipple. She was on the lazy side for sucking but she did really well. Just another process.

I threw away to memory lane the medicine bottle and lamb's nipple. This was a very exciting time not to have some of the many stares.

She was still cute and now the 4oz. bottle covered her whole face. How thrilling. We are making big progress in the nipple department and it's throw away time.

Along the way, Myracle never had a problem with food. Anything you wanted to put into her mouth she ate it. One would never have to force food down or coat the spoon with something sweet. Just say, okay, open up and sometimes this was done without asking. I tell you, this child was always ready to eat. Sometimes I wondered where it all goes- except when you would look at her pudgy stomach.

Oh, the precious moments and joy of happiness. The small things became more and more evident as she lived. No struggles; just strides. I am enjoying the happy times. She is fulfilling all of my dreams.

**Posing before the fall**

# 15 THREADS

## Surprise Trip

Myracle and I took off one weekend for a 5 hour trip to Mobile, Alabama. And to my surprise it was an experience. After carefully planning the stops to eat, change diapers and take medicine, we made a detour after 1 hour. It is raining cats and dogs and so are we. Myracle is wet, and wants a bottle, so I pull off the expressway to take care of her. I informed her, we can only take a thirty minute break and she sighs. I have to use the bathroom; in the rain… here we go…

Back in the car, she's secured in her car seat and we proceed. Two hours later it's time for more medicine, another twenty-minute stop. We burp and play for a few minutes and Myracle sleeps all the way home. It's truly amazing!

We had a blast with all of the family and Myracle did really well. Of course, she had her moments, always wanting to be held and rocked. There were enough arms to go around and I got some extra rest and sleep. It was a wonderful 3 day journey.

On our way back to Atlanta, she decides after thirty minutes she wants to get out of her car seat. I pulled over and calmly picked her up while attempting to make another adjustment. To my disbelief… she is now in my arms, strapped and I'm saying, you must be still because we could be stopped by the cops, so keep your head down.

Imagine this conversation. I set the cruise control and we drive for about 3.5 hours to a rest stop at the intersecting state line. I'm too tired and scared out of my wits for any words of comfort. We get out of the car, eat, walk and rest for about another thirty minutes while Myracle enjoys herself.

On the road again, buckled, fastened... on our way... still in the front seat. Now she begins to upchuck and boo-boo all over me, and of course on herself. I reach for anything in sight... that doesn't work, so we stop at the service station to get cleaned up. What an ordeal.

My thoughts, surely God is in this plan because I know this child must be tired. I proceed to put her in the car seat and pray to make it home within the next hour and a half... Lord, she sleeps.

At home, I'm too exhausted for words and she's snoring, one of her high marks. I called home upon my arrival to let everyone know we had made it safely but not without some excitement. Never again! I can't believe she did that to me and I am smiling.

Of course I trusted my "special child" to go on this trip... I tease, never again but perhaps I will again, only time will tell. I have told the story many times and I always get laughs from everyone. After all, what can't you expect from Myracle? She's got a gift.

## With a Child's Heart

"With a child's heart go face the worries of the day
With a child's heart turn each problem into play no need to worry
   no need to fear
Just being alive makes it all so very clear
With a child's heart nothing can ever get you down
With a child's heart you've got no reason to frown
Love is as welcome as a sunny sunny day
No grown-up thoughts to lead our hearts astray
Take life easy, so easy nice and easy,
The whole world smiles with you as you go your merry way
Oh with a child's heart, nothing's going to get me down."

*Michael Jackson*

# 16 THREADS

## *Punishment Tactics*

I am Myracle's mom and there were never any situations with her that frightened me. Had she been born PERFECT, my actions and reactions would be the same. Yes, I had to be cautious. I could not enforce too much punishment tactics because she was too fragile.

I remember putting her in the car seat and within minutes she wanted out. Or if she swings and it stops, guess what? She wants you to push again and again. Anytime you thought you were ahead of the game she would throw a wrench into the situation.

Let's not talk about going shopping; she would be wrapped up, around and under the hanging clothes at the department store. She was always moving in her little stroller and many times I had to catch her. Don't stand to look at something for one minute and she was gone. All you could say was shame on you. Lord, she knew how to capture your heart.

Myracle is always the winner! If there is a marathon she triumps.

> *"Sometimes the journey gets rough"*
>
> *Unknown*

**Myracle's visit to the
Martin Luther King Junior Center in Atlanta.**

# 17 THREADS

## Court Battle

I wrote Katie-Beckett Letters because another child was almost in the same state as Myracle. The appeal went to the reviewer's board for more studies. I carried Myracle for the hearing. As usual, she was quite charming. I had hoped there would be news coverage but they were not allowed to enter the room. I did not feel intimidated in the lease because I knew she had a sincere cause. The objective was to get her home. There was so much red tape. The provisions were to constitute 24 hour care, if accepted under the waiver.

On the other hand, a proposal for lesser service was submitted to the state for consideration. It was very difficult for "those in the system" to understand the health and wellbeing of Myracle and I was at their mercy. I firmly believe if one child can get a waiver, to be home with her family certainly Myracle was no exception.

As stated previously, this was a constitutional amendment. I was thought to be crazy when I challenged the legality under the Social Security Administration. To be such a fool, as they wanted me to believe, the so-called law now, no longer existed.

If this wasn't a blow to the ego, one could punch out my nose and pull away my ears. I could not believe I was actually hearing and seeing this humiliation.

I confidently worked with the social worker throughout this ordeal; later to discover the person was no longer with the system.

All sorts of efforts were made to locate the individual but to no avail. It seemed to be a shut and closed case; a mysterious disappearance with no likely clues. I thought about soliciting Angela Lansbury (Jessica Lang), Magnum P.I., Tom Selleck or Woodwar (Equalizer) McCall.

After two weeks of procrastination by the state, I finally received another case worker. The news was good; that I would be granted the waiver by certified mail. The enthusiasm was overwhelming and plans were made for Myracle's journey home.

To my "surprise" it was overturned in a matter of days and we were back to square one.

At this point, I'm devastated and humiliated to the utmost! I am just torn and equally as shattered as a mother. I am trying to relax in my state of depression. I am just tired of the lies. Hopefully, I will be able to sort out things more clearly.

I proceeded to ask for another appeal and sort of cool out. I drafted letters to the State, DHS and Congressmen and made telephone calls. I feel there has been a lot of unjust behavior toward's Myracle's cause.

I have more serious matters because Myracle has developed pneumonia. Her long term care for now was on the back burner.

She was hospitalized for a few days, monitored at home and she came out okay. I can't spend any more time fighting because she needs me to take care of her. There just aren't enough hours in the day. I am at the mercy of the doctors and the State. It is just another challenge and an impossible bridge to cross.

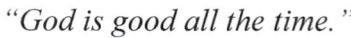

*"God is good all the time."*

_____*Psalms 21*

**Being a darling**

# 18 THREADS

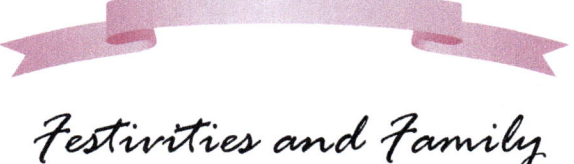

## *Festivities and Family*

It's the beginning of the festive season, Thanksgiving and Christmas. I am more than thankful and I know what is ahead of me will be more challenges. I will be delighted for the smiles, and all of the good cheer. Living on the edge is really hard to endure. So I am blessed to see the days come and go without heartache and pain.

Any justice done has been far removed from my mind at this time. The thoughts are still lingering in my head and I must make positively sure I am heading in the right direction for Myracle. I do believe in my heart of hearts that I have been poorly treated. And, I have learned also that many things are not what they appear or seem to be. Myracle was an innocent victim and the system wronged her in so many ways.

As devastating as it has been, I am learning to let go of all hard feelings. Myracle has begun to spring back. She keeps me hopeful with her constant demands (I am smiling and chuckling) and I am also taking deep breaths. Her medical levels were constant for two weeks and all is going pretty well.

Now I am hoping for some real joyous times during the holidays. I am trying not to get too excited because I am always on the edge with Myracle.

It is Thanksgiving and Myracle eats as much from my plate as I do. I am so proud of her appetite. I'm almost starved because whenever the fork goes near my mouth, somehow it ends up in her mouth. I am also exhausted. She is placed on the sofa to sit until I'm finished.

The little stinker behaves and goes to sleep for a little quickie. I'm truly amazed when she awakes with all smiles. I guess the tummy was full. How charming... That's really good because there are still a few more days with family. She makes it all worthwhile.

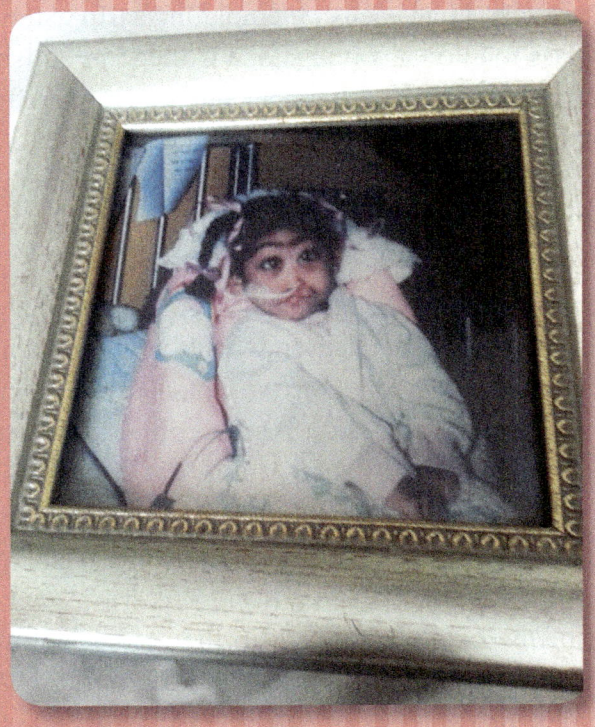

**Myracle's last hospital visit**

# 19 THREADS

*Feeling Guilty*

With crisis after crisis for a few months, I felt stretched beyond my capacity. I had been contemplating a trip without Myracle to my 20th class reunion at Livingstone College in Salisbury, North Carolina and decided, not, with much contemplation. After all, I had never spent a weekend away from her and this felt scary. Not trusting anyone caused me great concern and I would be about 4 1/2 hours away. Lord, how could I do this? I have NEVER been away from her.

Finally, with much guilt, I decided to go. I left all hotel numbers at the center and with several friends who would be able to locate me if anything happened. Upon my arrival, at school, I immediately called and several other times during the trip because I did not feel secure about leaving her. My reservations got the best of me. There were second guesses. How could I meet with my classmates and feel happy? It took such a long time to have a child, and most people knew about Myracle; the special gift.

Several of my classmates were in the medical profession and comforted me during the festivities. I still felt guilty but we talked about the problems.

It was very encouraging knowing my friends cared personally

and guided me professionally. I tried to relax but I had a lot on my mind.

One of the doctors in my class worked directly with the State and knew my actions to proceed were just. Another classmate had lost a child as a result of brain damage. Unfortunate for them their child only survived a couple of months, and yet they were encouraging.

The reunion is just about over and before leaving many of us got together for breakfast. Gus, a friend, classmate and doctor told me what a wonderful mom I was and that Myracle would be alright and not to feel guilty. That was hard to swallow beneath the tears rolling down my face, into my omelet. They understood and so did I... life goes on but the memory is always there. The words were good and the friendship was even better.

Being around such sensitive classmates was a relief. Although the pain was in my heart, I knew all would be well. I packed up and headed to Atlanta with no road problems. The first place I stopped was to see my baby, who received me wide eyed. We hugged, kissed, walked and talked for a few hours until it was time to go to bed. She had done well over the week-end without me, but I knew better.

It was very unusual for Myracle to be at the center on the week-end.

Everybody asked why she was there because they knew her mom would always pick her up. They asked where her mom is . Where had I gone? Yes, this was a very frightening decision but I had faith.

Somehow I just got the feeling it was time to trust her for a change because she could get into crisis mode in a second and everybody and everything would be frantic. I am feeling really guilty.

> *"I have shewed you all things, how that so laboring ye ought to support the weak, and to remember the words of the Lord Jesus, how he said, It is more blessed to give than to receive."*
>
> Acts 20: 35

**Myracle as a big girl**

# 20 THREADS

## *It is Christmas*

Before any plans can be executed, Myracle must get her checkup from the doctor. Then, I must submit her holiday schedule to the center. She would be with me for three (3) weeks. Gee, there were so many loops including the preparation for medical regiments for the entire trip. And, what's with all of the ifs?

Myracle received her clearance to travel. We were off and on our way to Mobile for most of the holidays. It seems, every time we go home, we are asked, if we came to stay, like forever? Of course, it's stuff for Myracle. There are syringes, food, diapers, bottles, nipples, medicines, feeders, clothes and toys.

This time there is also a car seat and her wheel chair and of course her special seat that was tailored to her body. This seat helps to safely strap her, in case there were seizures. My God, it was a lot to carry anywhere.

I answered the inquiring minds and said, we are just here for Christmas. Aside from Myracle's stuff there were also presents for everybody. It was more than you could imagine. We were the Santa and Claus, with all of the helpers as well, except for the red and white trim of the Santa dress and beard.

Nothing mattered to Myracle because she now had more arms and laps to hold her. Yeah, it's really Christmas and the fun is about to begin.

*"Without a struggle,
there can be no progress."*

*Frederick Douglass*

**Birthday party**

# 21 THREADS

## *Ribbons and Pearls*

The triumphs were large and Myracle was gifted. Her impact upon my life created many bright and sunny days. Even when it seemed dark, she would just give you that spark and the little smiles would come. Sometimes I struggled with fear but soon realized I needed to be strong because Myracle needed me and I needed her too.

This was more than a 2 –way street. I chose not to be a wimp because there was too much at stake and the road was very, very rocky.

In times of distress, Myracle was always in charge and bouncing back from one crisis episode to another. Sometimes I would just talk to her and say, please…NO, Myracle ! Sometimes it resonated but other times not. Most of the time, I just gave up and fell into her cue. No matter what defense you took, she always had the last say.

Just watching her everyday was such a blessing. Through any and all thoughts of pain, Myracle made you forget how special she was. The challenges with her were surreal. All I could think about was being encouraged. I knew from which my strength came from and only heaven and earth were my thoughts.

I prayed every day for courage... and today as I reflect, I am able to sustain anything, any person, circumstance, place, or thing. The people, places and activities of my life is a testament to what I endured with Myracle. Her threads have now been woven into bright ribbons and pearls.

Her stresses became my passion. It was a piece of cake and all encompassing. I have found that life has afforded many pleasantries because she lived against all odds.

On February 7, 1986, Myracle was quite feverish. It was really not unusual. I filled the bathtub with water so that her body could cool off. Due to her "irregularities" with her hypothalamus she often spiked a temperature or over heated in her body... It always "worked" but not this time. The ambulance was called because she was not responding to the cool down. She was rushed to the hospital and all of her doctors were summoned to the hospital. After a short while her doctors arrived.

I had lived life well and Myracle was a jewel. I spoke to the doctors and asked that they not try to perform any miraculous measures. Myracle tried her best to beat the odds. Her time was coming to an end. The threads that were ribbons are now pearls. The hospital did their best. Her destiny was clear.

The medical team brought her to me. She was fragile. I took her into the fold of my left arm and she took her last breath at 10:43am.

It was emotional and very heart wrenching. I remember it as if it was yesterday. I live with those constant memories. Not a day goes by that I don't think about that moment. I am thankful that I have the strength to smile!

Making her arrangements were very, very difficult. I knew she had been my gift and her life expectancy was uncertain. I used every day of her life as well as mine to make more wishes happen because she knew how much I loved her.

My family and friends were called. She had a little white basinet for a casket. It was the smallest I had ever seen. I did not want anyone to dress her, so I took on that task because I wanted her to look so...we forgot the pamper, so I located one in the car. She looked like an angel with that long adorning curly braid. Just so...??????

A day before the service, I remember my daddy Leo saying that he did not want anyone to cut up (act unruly). So, he made sure all of the little children in the family had a chance to go to the funeral home. And yes, they made several trips back and forth.

Every time somebody started to cry at the house, he would say, take them back to the funeral home to see Myracle. When Daddy spoke everybody listened. God blessed all of us during that time.

On the day of the service, February 11, 1986, it was a bitter cold day with threats of snow. We managed...

Myracle is buried at Southview Cemetery, Garden of the Good Shepard, #7, Atlanta, Georgia.

I frequent often and find that her birthday and Mother's Day are the times that really have become very special for me. My saying now is that every day we breathe, we rejoice for another day.

Myracle had 21 months and 7 days...her journey ended on earth. She is in HEAVEN and my heart aches...

**Mom's visit to grave site**

# Myracle Juel Cannon

General Nature:

1. Good
2. Eats cereal and all foods. Has not developed any preferences at this point in her life.
3. Enjoys music
4. Smiles and shows all 32's (she only had 4 teeth)
5. Appears to have good hearing perception
6. Active; moves body and head frequently.
7. Will stiffen body often
8. Likes to have people talk to her
9. Loves being held and rocked
10. Becomes constipated easily; usually given Baby Lax suppositories to soften stools or relieve constipation.
11. Prefers food over milk.
12. Drinks water with no problem.
13. Becomes irritable easily.
14. Will not go to sleep on her own unless she's given a few bounces.
15. Stays awake almost all night.
16. Enjoys stroller rides inside and outside
17. When she's moving she is most happy.
18. Enjoys her swing.
19. Likes musical toys

20. Sleeps during the day; almost 2.5 to 4 hours at one time
21. Prefers sleeping on her side, NEVER place her on her back unless changing her diaper.
22. Her bed must be elevated at all times.
23. Likes to get her hair washed.
24. Enjoys baths and always moves excessively in water.
25. Formula sometimes has to be pumped into her.

# Seizure Activity

1. Moves hands up, then down becoming lethargic with grunts and then smiles
2. Eyes move up and around sometimes.
3. Often screams; grab hands and cuddle to muffle sound and scary feeling (I practiced this routine to talk her out of having the seizure)

# *Formula*

Isomil ready to feed

Feedings:

Normally cereal in the am
Vegetables, dessert, etc., mid-day
Bottles, fix 3-4 ounces
Water, any amount
More vegetables
Cereal at night after her first nap
10:30pm and sometimes 1am- 2am depending upon when she awakes.
Another bottle

# *Medications*

1. Myracle takes all medications through the syringe; normally tolerates very well.
2. To avoid throwing up, medications must be taken daily.

Notes:
1. Give phenobarbital, first
2. "Dilantin, Second
3. "Tegratol and synthroid (combined)
   This allows for her tongue to cool off; otherwise she will in most cases not tolerate.
4. If she is given water or milk immediately before her medications everything will come up!
5. Vitamins must be given in cereal.

NOTE: DO NOT HESISTATE TO CALL MOM ANYTIME!!!!

# Special Notes

1. Mom will do all laundry
2. Pick up Myracle up every Saturday morning unless notified
3. Do not let her get away with murder during feedings. PLEASE!!
4. She needs to try and maintain all that she's got and more.

# *Myracle's Party, April 27, 1985*

| Gifts | Giver |
|---|---|
| 1. Happy Apple | Christopher |
| 2. Yellow panties, ball & rattle | Ms. Mary |
| 3. $1.00. | Omar |
| 4. $5.00 | Talia |
| 5. $5.00 | Lawren |
| 6. Pink, yellow & blue 2 piece w/ pink flowers | Morgan |
| 7. Red, white & blue 2 piece | Liz |
| 8. Blue & white polka dot w/ red rick rack border | Quentin |
| 9. Red & white seersucker eyelet jumpsuit/ | Joyce |
| 10. Lavender & white 2 piece | Minnie |
| 11. Pink & white polka dot dress | Barbara |
| 12. Buster Brown Lavender &white jumpsuit | Marian |
| 13. Pink &white seersucker 2 piece | Chubby |
| 14. Nannette pink &white dress w/ orange overlay | Nanny Joyce |
| 15. Pink & white lace & ribbon socks | Nanny Joyce |
| 16. Strawberry 2 piece | Shirley |
| 17. Pink & white, yellow & blue, 2 piece | Vera |

# Acknowledgements

*"How far you go in the life depends on your being tender with the young, compassionate with the aged, sympathetic with the striving and tolerant of the weak and strong. Because someday in your life you will have been all of these."*

*George Washington Carver*

# Epilogue

Myracle's Journey was meant to be. I carried her to full term enduring pain for nine months. Only God knew what was ahead of me. When he gifted me to "birth" my path was perfectly CLEAR. Of course, not to me but it was evident. I followed all of Dr. Borders' orders to the letter. From the beginning of the pregnancy I was flat on my back for three months and again at seven months because Myracle was posing a threat. In my heart of hearts, I do believe she was threatening to abort, I had to be extra careful for her safety as well as my own.

I was hospitalized many times. Myracle was stable, and determined to be… and I welcomed that blessing. Feeling the power of her love inside of me gave me more determination to be careful. I proceeded with a cautious attitude. When she kicked, I kicked back; to let her know we were in this battle together. There was never any sign of trouble ahead.

My heart knew she wanted me to be her mother. There were no tests to perform and to think anything was remotely wrong other than she was something feisty. Nothing indicted she would be retarded and even today, holoprosencephaly (HPE) cannot be seen or detected in a fetus. This cranio facial an anomaly is something that happens. Scientists believe that HPE is an environmental factor. I have spent many hours searching and there is not enough strength to continue the journey. Myrcale is at peace and so am I.

Today, none of this really matters, Myracle outlived the odds and brought, peace, joy, love and hope to me. She knew how "special" she was... I always said "she got away with murder." I feel free, no sorrow for allowing me to be who and what I am TODAY. I am strengthened for all of my yesterdays and truly blessed. More children were not possible, so I love upon all of my siblings, nieces, nephews, god-children, students, anybody else and of course my dog, Mardi.

Life is good. Thanks to all in the village!

# Special Acknowledgements

Southwest Hospital
Egleston Hospital
Shaw Temple A. M. E. Zion Church
Livingstone College, Class of 1970
CH2M Hill Engineers
Dr. Joyce Marley Ball


I needed a "village" for support and it was always available. Some days and nights were dim, but I could always feel that glimmer of love and hope.

I am truly blessed by all of your love and support.

Quotes have been used in this book to illustrate a holistic approach to describing Myracle's Journey. It is hoped you will find favor in the words and phrases.

She was born fractured by the threads…struggled and survived with ribbons and pearls of love and grace to the bitter end. Her legacy will always be with me. She gave me her heart and I gave her my everlasting love.

# About The Author

Regina Woodard Cannon was born in Mobile, Alabama and completed her studies at St. Elmo High School, St. Elmo, Alabama; B.A. Livingstone College, Salisbury, North Carolina and M. L. S. Atlanta University, Atlanta, Georgia.

Her professional career included public libraries, government institutes, corporate, business, non-profit, law, engineering and agriculture.

She spends quality time with her family (six sisters), while also traveling, ushering at many of the popular venues around town, dancing, genealogy research, reading biographies, worshipping in church activities at Spread the Word, exercising, singing, practicing sign language, spoiling students, water aerobics, writing and anything else that keeps her moving. And of course keeping up with her precious dog, Mardi.

After retirement she returned to her hometown, Coden, Alabama (26 miles south of Mobile) to relax along the seashore, enjoy the wonderful seafood, spend quality time with family and continue to travel. The adventure continues and life is fantastic!

She is also writing another book entitled "Seven".

CPSIA information can be obtained at www.ICGtesting.com
Printed in the USA
BVOW11*0646281015

424525BV00001B/2/P

9 781478 762294